IT IS DONE!

IT IS DONE!

The Final Step To Instant Manifestations

RICHARD DOTTS

© Richard Dotts 2014
2nd edition
ISBN-13: 9781519125422
ISBN-10: 1519125429
Questions / comments? The author can be contacted at
RichardDotts@gmail.com

TABLE OF CONTENTS

An Important Message from
Richard Dotts · · · · · · · · · · · · vii

Chapter One   My Personal Adventures with
Manifestation · · · · · · · · · · · · · · · 1

Chapter Two   This Finally Made the
Difference for Me · · · · · · · · · · · 10

Chapter Three   How the Answer
I Needed Was Shown to Me · · · 19

Chapter Four   The Tale of Two Students · · · · · 28

Chapter Five   Unseen Blocks That Delay Your
Manifestations · · · · · · · · · · · · · 37

Chapter Six   The Universe Has No
Ulterior Motive · · · · · · · · · · · · 49

Chapter Seven   The Significance
of "It Is Done!" · · · · · · · · · · · · · 58

Chapter Eight   The "It Is Done"
Process in Detail · · · · · · · · · · · 68

Chapter Nine   Using "It Is Done" in Other
Situations · · · · · · · · · · · · · · · · 77

About The Author · · · · · · · · · · 85

An Introduction to the
Manifestations Approach
of Richard Dotts · · · · · · · · · · · 87
Other Books by Richard Dotts · 93

An Important Message from Richard Dotts

In this book, I share a powerful manifestation technique called the "It Is Done" technique, which can greatly multiply the effectiveness of any manifestation process you are currently using. The beauty of the "It Is Done" technique is that it perfectly complements whatever manifestation process you are using, be it visualization, meditation, or even just a stating of intentions. This is the technique that I use myself on a regular basis.

Readers may be tempted to skip the first part of this book and go straight to the second part, where I outline the technique in detail and its various applications. Please resist the urge to do so, because the technique <u>may not work for you</u> without sufficient background knowledge. It is very important that you first grasp the principles I talk about in the first half of this book on the 4 major manifestation blocks that hold most people back. It took me years to realize that I had these blocks myself, but the moment I removed these blocks, things happened very quickly and spontaneously for me even without using any specific technique in particular.

Therefore, what I'm saying is that you will get a whole lot of benefit just by reading the first half of this book alone...but your gains will be much reduced if you omit the first half and skip to the second half directly. There is a reason why the book is written in this order, which will become even clearer to you once you truly understand the whole process.

I wish you all the best in your manifestations and in your creative journey. And may you be filled with a deep sense of peace in everything you do. Enjoy the ride!

Richard Dotts (RichardDotts@gmail.com)

CHAPTER ONE

MY PERSONAL ADVENTURES WITH MANIFESTATION

When it comes to working with the creative laws of the Universe, there are generally two groups of people. The first group picks up these principles very quickly, and they are soon able to manifest their desired lives and conditions at will. The second group takes a longer time to internalize these principles, and often a period of struggle ensues before they are able to see results in their lives. When they finally do see results however, the effects can be sporadic and temporary. They often find themselves regressing back to their old selves and old belief systems, or doing something to sabotage whatever results they have obtained. Many people in the second group never reach their desired states of success and fulfillment, and those who manage to achieve some kind of a breakthrough do so only after a long time.

I would love to say that I belong to the first group, the group that can pick up and use these manifestation principles and laws at will. When people look at me today, they are often surprised by how eloquently I teach these principles through my books, and by my practical understanding of these laws. What many people do not know about is my ten-year "struggle" with the manifestation process, where I spent ten long years trying to learn and apply all of these Universal laws—with few results.

If you identify with the second group, rest assured that you are certainly not alone and that you *can* change the situation. I spent ten years stumbling over possibly every single pitfall, and dealing with possibly every single insecurity so that you do **not** have to go down the same path I did. Take my story as a testimony that it is just as possible for you as well. In times where I could not keep up the faith, I often turned to the great spiritual masters and teachers for guidance and assurance. Their teachings helped to keep my faith alive in the darkest hours.

The purpose of writing these books on manifestation and creating your own reality—and more broadly, the Law of Attraction—is to share what I have learned with others such that they do not have to make the same mistakes that I did. As I look back on my journey today, I realize that the struggle is always optional. The belief of "no pain, no gain", or that you have to "struggle" before you achieve something worthwhile is just that—another pervasive belief borne out of our human conditioning. As I look back today, I realize that had I known what I know today, I could have cut through all that mess

and clutter. I would not have taken all those unnecessary detours, or kept circling around the same
spot. I would have been able to identify all of my
self-sabotaging thought patterns, and move beyond
them quickly and effortlessly.

And yet, if you ask me today whether I would
give all of that up—my answer would be a surpris-
ing "no." Spiritual understanding, once attained,
cannot be taken away from you. For some people,
spiritual understanding comes through inspiration
and through direct knowing, which is the way I tend
to receive guidance and nudges nowadays. I just
receive them in my awareness, and then go along
with the flow. This is the way we have all been made
to function, which is to always be guided along what
I call the "flow of life." For others, spiritual understanding comes through overcoming problems and
obstacles, and learning lessons from them. They
bang their heads around a problem or life situation
for as long as they can, before they finally see the
light of it all or the futility of it all. Either way, spiritual enlightenment occurs when they finally learn
their lessons. When they finally learn their lesson,
the outer circumstances and problems dissolve,
because they are no longer needed. Once you have
learned what is needed for your evolution, the outer
situation changes—because you no longer need the
situation to be your teacher.

Most people have to learn through the second method before they finally learn through the
first method. The reason is in the education and

conditioning we have received from our youth. We have been taught to be extremely skeptical and wary of anything that spontaneously wells up within us, and only to accept external sources of guidance that can be independently validated and verified. In other words, we have been taught the importance of getting our knowledge through indirect, third-party sources, instead of from within ourselves. But as I have realized, along with so many others, there *is* a wellspring of knowledge and intelligence within yourself that far exceeds whatever source of knowledge is on the outside. You can learn to tap into this well-spring for guidance and everlasting abundance.

I am often asked why I put so much effort into the study of these Universal principles and laws. Another related question is whether it is "selfish" to focus so much on manifestations, or creating abundance and prosperity. Those who are exposed to these teachings for the first time often feel guilty when the good starts flowing into their lives, and when they see those around them not experiencing it. They can't believe that life is so easy for them!

My response is always the same. A greater understanding of these Universal principles and laws lets us function in a way in which we are supposed to. It is the only natural way for us. Life is supposed to be easy. Life is supposed to be creative, fun and effortless. We are here to create and to see our creations to fruition, and then to create some more. We are not here to experience struggle, sorrow or pain on our path to creation. When you realize that life is supposed to be fun, enjoyable and about living up to your highest potential, you'll suddenly become an avid student of these laws, because at their very basis, these Universal Laws are about just that—living the good life.

A good life is a creative life. A good life is an abundant life. A good life is when you're in flow, bouncing happily from one moment to the next, from one achievement to the next. If any problems or obstacles crop up along the way, you deal with them quickly and easily and then go on your way. You do not remain stuck on them, or allow yourself to be hung up by them long after the moment is over. A good life just flows, and is a never-ending series of happy moments.

The most effective way I've found to teach others how to have a good life is by not framing my teachings as such. I don't start off by saying, "I'm here to teach you how to lead a good life." That would sound too grandiose and too impossible. So instead I say, "I'm here to teach you how to create and to get the things you want." Now that sounds more possible. It sounds more immediate and achievable. But implicit in that understanding is also a profound truth: When you learn how to create even just one thing at will in your life, you can repeat the process over and over again to "create" many other things— until all of the conditions in your life match up with the desired conditions. Therefore, tapping your powers to create even a single, small thing is a very powerful step along your journey. We have all been gifted with the powers to do so, and my work merely guides you towards doing so.

I now look upon my journey as an adventure, because of the many struggles and fun times I've had along the way. Again, I must remind you that the struggles are optional. It does not mean that you have to go through the exact same learning curve I did, just because it was what I went through. Looking back, I now know that I had to go through such a steep learning curve because I had to overcome and undo the training I received from my formal, scientific education—as well as the general deep distrust and lack of faith I had in these Universal matters. Had I magically been able to remove these two elements of distrust and fear from my life right from the start, I would have been able to achieve what I have, a hundred times faster. So once again, let me remind you that any struggle is always optional.

Your Manifestation Abilities Lie Within You

A meaningful way to look at our manifestation and creative powers is as such: all of us have been imbued with these abilities. They are present in each and every individual human being, with no exceptions. However, on top of these abilities lie a lot of weeds and unwanted stuff—things such as our negative conditioning, our negative beliefs, our negative thoughts…all of this unwanted junk is heaped over the treasure below, which is our true manifestation abilities.

Most people look at these manifestation abilities as something we have to "acquire." That's why they are so concerned about whether they are "doing" the right thing, or taking the right steps to send their requests for material things to the Universe. On the flip side, expensive books / courses / seminars and a whole myriad of self-help products have sprung up offering to teach individuals how to get as much as they can out of this Universal automated teller machine. "If only you put in a request the right way..." or "If only you ask in this five-step manner...", then something will happen and the Universe will respond to your request.

Immediately one can see how this model or belief system differs from the one I shared earlier. These people are telling you that these manifestation abilities and skills need to be *acquired.* They need to be learned. That was what I initially believed too, which is why I spent so much time and effort making sure I was doing the steps correctly. Whenever I read a book, I would worry about whether I was following the instructions properly—and I would keep doing the steps over and over again, just to be sure that the "Universe" out there would get my requests clearly.

Over time, I discovered that this wasn't an accurate representation of how the Universe really functioned. I made this revelation after discovering that I still received certain things or conditions in my life despite not "asking" for them in conventional ways. At other times, I did not even need to "ask," for the manifestation was preceded by my asking! It was as if the Universe knew exactly what I needed even before I did, and delivered it right to me in perfect timing and harmony.

This book and my teachings are really geared towards this school of thought. You'll find that I place very little emphasis on *how* you ask for something, because in my experience, it simply *does not matter*. You are asking for your desired conditions whether you know it or not. You are asking whether you put it in words or not. You are asking whether you put it into pictures or not. You are always doing the asking—because *creating* IS the asking. When one creates, one asks! However, the issue is whether you are clearing enough of the gunk away such that you allow what you are asking to come into your life. That gunk we are talking about includes negative beliefs, negative conditioning, worry, and fear thoughts and doubts. Any of these will stand between you and your manifestations.

Therefore, if you find a way to deal with all these negatives—your negative conditioning, worries or fears and make them disappear once and for all (or at least greatly reduce their frequency). You'll find miraculous things start happening for you left, right and center! You'll find manifestations and demonstrations occurring for you **even before** you ask for them. You do not even have to deliberately *ask* for much, because you'll find that the Universe rises up perfectly to meet your need every single time—and it is only after the fact that you realize the wonderful perfection of this Universe. But it would not be possible to reach this state of awareness until you are fully clean and clear, until you fully remove all the roadblocks standing between your current reality and your true abilities.

So don't worry about whether you are a good manifestor, or whether you are able to create your own desired life. The difference between the first and second group of people I shared at the beginning of this chapter lies *not* in the lack of abilities in the latter, but because people in the latter group are constantly blocking their own manifestations through thoughts of fear, worry and doubt. Remove them, and you will permanently remove all blocks that stand between you and a better life. These blocks therefore, are always self-imposed and put in place by your own limited perceptions. And it is my sincere intention to show you how to break past them in the remainder of this book. Remember the insights that came to me during meditation one night, which I've proven to be true since: "Remove your worries, and your manifestations will come very quickly!"

Chapter Two

This Finally Made the Difference for Me

To an individual who is accustomed to worrying, worrying seems like the most natural thing in the world to do. If the previous sentence sounds painfully obvious, stick with me for a moment, because I have a much deeper point to illustrate. This principle, if understood, will make your manifestation journey easier.

Back when I was first exposed to all these Universal principles about creating one's own reality, I was a chronic worrier. I probably inherited this trait from my mother, who was a compulsive worrier as well. She saw the need to plan for every possible contingency in advance, and to be prepared for every possible scenario that could happen. While this trait made her well-prepared most of the time, it also made her unnecessarily stressful and jumpy, always ready to snap at the first sign of a problem. Needless to say, she did not enjoy activities with a high degree of ambiguity like taking a vacation, because her overwhelming need to plan and to know how everything would work out in advance hampered her from enjoying the present moment. I believe that she has enjoyed very few moments in her life.

For a long time, I was just like that as well. I thought that *worrying* was the only natural thing to do! As a result of my incessant "worrying," I did very well in school. By most outside standards I was "successful," at least judging by my "achievements." And yet I was still unhappy, because all my achievements were driven largely by worries and fears. I walked around with a deep sense of worry and fear that I would do badly and somehow let everyone down around me. Even when I was doing well, I was worried that someday it would all come to an end and everyone around me would be disappointed. You can see how I was living in a self-perpetuated, negative cycle. I was literally a nervous wreck! I assumed that just because I was constantly worrying about the past, present and future in my head (my own inner world), that everyone else was the same and would do the same, too! Therefore, my own beliefs and mental conditioning clouded my view of the world. I could not even imagine an alternative inner world because I thought everyone functioned in the same way I did.

Now this is the important point I'm trying to make—**it is the same for you as well**. Up until this point in your life, you have been living under a set of presumptions and beliefs. Some of them may serve you, while others (such as worrying) may not. Whether these beliefs serve you or otherwise, all of these presumptions and beliefs will seem entirely logical and sound to you at this very moment. They are what you have believed in your entire life. The way you do things in your inner world, your inner state of mind will all seem very natural and familiar to you right now. You cannot even begin to fathom a new way of functioning or operating in this world that is *different* from what you have always been accustomed to.

Since worrying was such a pervasive thing for me, I could not stop myself from doing it. I didn't even *know* I was constantly worrying, because to me, it felt logical that one had to think about the future and make plans for it! I could not imagine people going through life without worrying about anything. To me, they seemed irresponsible. I now know that many people function in the world with a deep sense of faith and trust in the Universe, who are in turn richly provided for by the Universe. This, as I have mentioned before in my previous books, is not a sign of naivety or recklessness, but actually one of true spiritual maturity.

I am not advocating that we stop caring about the people and things around us. What I am advocating, and what will be clearer as this book progresses, is that there is a difference between being "concerned" and "worried." I am generally a careful person, and when I travel overseas for example, I am concerned about my safety and well-being. This means taking all the necessary precautions and steps to protect myself and to safeguard my belongings.

It may mean purchasing travel insurance. However, beyond taking a few precautionary steps, I do not worry incessantly about the risks involved. I do not keep dwelling on the things that can wrong when I go on my trip. I accept that the risks are there, and then "let go and trust" in the Universe. Once we have taken all the steps humanly possible, it is time for us to let go and to let the Universe do the rest. The Universe cannot possibly do its magic with us intervening all the time.

Little did I know that these worrying feelings in general were preventing my manifestations from happening. Therefore, no matter what I did on the outside (visualize, affirm, meditate, use vision boards, write down my intentions) or how many times I performed those actions—my success was only sporadic at best. I mistakenly pinpointed my lack of results on the fact that I lacked the knowledge in this area, or that I was not doing the right stuff or using the right "methods." In fact, the real **and only** problem was my worrying. A worry thought is a counter intention that effectively focuses all of our energies on the unwanted, and therefore perpetuates the unwanted! The short answer is that if I had found a way to quit worrying back then, I would have solved all of my problems *and* stumbled upon the "secret" to manifestation I was trying so hard to find.

But I did not find it for another ten years. Not because I was not smart enough or not trying hard enough, but because I didn't even realize that I was worrying or thinking negative thoughts most of the time! Whenever I read about the detrimental effects of worrying in self-help or spiritual books (such as when a book like this one explained that worrying would delay our manifestations), I found a perfectly good reason to rationalize my behavior away. I reasoned that I wasn't a compulsive worrier (I was), and that I only worried about "reasonable" or logical stuff. That in itself is a misconception, because *any* kind of worrying hampers our manifestations, whether they are on the same subject as our desires or otherwise. This means that there is no need to worry specifically about "money" to keep "money" away, because *any* kind of worry produces negative resistance that keeps us away from our good in general. Now you can see why this trap is so difficult to get out of—because it does require that we break free from our current levels of awareness to see beyond it.

Another reason I used to rationalize my worrying is that I was doing lots of the "positive" stuff, including visualizations, meditations, affirmations and "feeling good" on the side. I was reading so many positive thinking and self-help books that I could quote and recite paragraphs from memory! Little did I know that I was only feeling good for a relatively small part of the day (for example, when I was actively reading those books), as compared to the majority of the time, when I was incessantly worrying.

Therefore, I am willing to wager that if manifestations have been slow in coming for you, it is your

ongoing thoughts that are blocking them. Most of these thoughts will seem so "natural" and logical to you, that you do not even notice they are there. You may even try to argue against their very existence, or think that they are life-affirming for you. Thankfully, there is an easy way to change all of this, and it starts with having a conscious *awareness*.

Your Current Results Cannot Lie
There is a quick and easy way to see if your ongoing thoughts serve you, and that is to look at the current **results** in your life. The results you get in your physical reality never lie. They are **always in direct response** to your feelings and thoughts about a particular subject. There are no exceptions. Any time you perceive a "lack" in any area of your life, it is because you are thinking corresponding "lack" thoughts within yourself (or *feeling* corresponding lack *feelings*).

Sometimes, a person can seem to be very positive and upbeat on the outside, but remember that we live in a vibrational Universe, and the Universe always picks up on your thoughts, one hundred percent of the time. Therefore, you may fool those around you, but **not** the Universe, which always knows your true vibrations on any subject. It is for this reason that you should not let other people's opinions of yourself affect you. What they can observe is only based on your outer-projected reality which is a very small part of you, and not an accurate representation of your entire inner reality, which is what the Universe picks up on. I have long told myself to disregard the opinions and thoughts of others, especially their thoughts and expectations of me, because those have **absolutely nothing** to do with creating my reality. The only time another person's opinions can affect your reality is when you let those thoughts influence you, thereby affecting your own thoughts about the subject. But why take the hard way? Why wait for someone to "motivate" or "de-motivate" you? Focus on managing your *own* vibrations, your own feelings and your *own* expectations. In a nutshell, that is everything you have to do to create your own reality—and nothing else matters.

Here's the "secret" (if there ever was one)—you can change your thoughts and feelings in an instant. You can go from lackful and limited thinking in one instant, to abundant and prosperous thinking the next. Nothing and no one out there is stopping you from doing so. But there is an additional step required, and that is to *remain there in this new state of consciousness.* You need to stay there and immerse yourself in the new reality you have chosen for yourself. The purpose of this whole book and the next few chapters is to teach you how to do so. It is not enough to stay in this new reality that you have chosen for just sporadic and short periods of time throughout the day, and then revert back to fear-based thinking for most of the time. Once you have managed to shift yourself into this new state of awareness and consciousness, you need to make sure that you stay there for as long as possible. This is the only secret, and perhaps the only requirement to making the whole thing "work."

Do not feel discouraged if you are constantly worried or thinking negative thoughts most of the time. As I mentioned earlier, the first step you need to take is to develop an *awareness* of the issue. By reading this book, you are bringing this issue to your attention and thus to your conscious awareness. Once this is in your conscious awareness, you can then take active steps to change it.

Just for the next half a day or so, really take a close look at and scrutinize your thoughts. Not just your thoughts in general, but what goes on in your mind most of the time, every single day. Pick up each thought and examine it. Does it serve you? Is it a fear-based, negative thought or is it a positive thought? Be really honest with yourself and give up any excuses for the negative ones. As I mentioned, negative conditioning is so pervasive in our society that we do not even notice our negative thoughts more than half of the time! We do not even notice that we have all been conditioned to think negatively, and constant negative thought is the number one roadblock to quick and effective manifestations.

I would like to say that I stumbled upon a magic pill* that changed things overnight for me and caused me to stop worrying immediately after popping it, but things were certainly not so! Instead, things happened in a much better and cooler way than I ever could have imagined, through a series of serendipitous events that happened over a period of time…

(*Note: There are pills and supplements commonly available that claim to relieve stress and lift your mood. I'm not talking about prescription drugs like anti-depressants, but supplements sold over the counter. One of the common ingredients in these supplements is L-Theanine, an amino acid found to boost one's mood, and is naturally found in tea. I do **not** recommend taking these supplements to improve your mood, as you'll soon find that they do little to curb your worrying if you are a chronic worrier. A pill cannot change the content of your thoughts! While you may feel better, the change is chemically-induced and not the result of a conscious, deliberate intention from the inside out. It is way more powerful and beneficial to learn how to directly control your thoughts using the tips and techniques outlined in these books, rather than to wait for a pill to do it for you.)

Chapter Three

How the Answer I Needed Was Shown to Me

The insights and realizations you are reading about in this book did not come to me overnight. While I may write about them and teach them here in a very coherent manner, understand that they came to me over long periods of study and observation. At various points in my life, I observed the manifestations that worked and at other times, I observed the unwanted manifestations in my life and traced them back to the very thoughts and feelings that produced them. By doing this consistently over a period of several years, I began to understand the underlying thought patterns that created recurring events and results in my life.

For the first ten years, while I was studying these Universal Laws, I applied them in a very superficial manner. I treated the exercises and techniques as "spells" or "processes," something to be repeated over and over again, with the hope that something would work for me. As a result, I tried many different techniques, often hopping from one program to another, with the hope of finding a more powerful technique than the last. Sometimes the techniques worked, but mostly they did not. When the techniques did work, the results they produced were largely sporadic—and I often found myself regressing into my old states of being.

This regression and "moving backwards" into square one became a recurring theme in my life. We all have recurring themes in our lives; some of them are good (desired) and some of them are bad (unwanted). Whenever you observe a negative, unwanted recurring theme in your life, there is a high chance that some recurring negative thought pattern is producing it. Fortunately, any recurring thought pattern (a belief) is just that—a recurring thought—and these can be consciously changed at any time. However, you must *be* the one initiating the change and not depend on anything external (such as a pill, or someone else) to do it for you.

In my case, the recurring thought patterns were thoughts of fear and worry. I constantly worried about whether there was going to be enough, and how I was going to make my next dollar to pay for my expenses. I was so afraid of running out of money. These fears and worries became so deeply ingrained in me that I did not even realize they were there—because I could not see them clearly for what they were—simple beliefs that could be changed at any time. The fundamental fear of "running out of money" produced a deep motivational drive for me to earn more money, and to strive for more. Therefore, what I could observe was only my conscious behavior of "striving" for more, and not the deep fear that was beneath everything.

Once I recognized and then let go of this deep, underlying fear pattern (the simple belief that I would run out of money and have bad things happen to me), everything dissolved by itself and changed literally overnight. Suddenly, money began to pour in from every possible source—and as miraculous as it sounds, money often came *into* my bank accounts even **before** I recognized the need! For the first time in my life, I understood what Jesus of Nazareth was trying to convey more than 2,000 years ago when he said, "Before you ask I will answer, and while you are yet speaking I shall give it unto thee." Again, I am making a biblical reference here because it is the most familiar and most easily accessible text for most readers, but you'll find ancient masters across other spiritual traditions saying essentially the same thing.

Before You Ask, It Shall Be Given

Just the other day, I accepted a project that paid a certain sum of money. Not long after receiving the payment, I realized that the payment covered the exact sum of money needed for a magazine subscription I was planning to purchase for quite some time, essentially making my subscription "free." A gift had fallen into my lap, just like that! The Universe met my wants exactly, without me even having to consciously ask for it!

I am recounting these actual experiences to show you what is possible when you have a deep sense of faith and trust in the Universe. I have often said that when you have such a profound sense of faith and trust in the Universe, that no proof is necessary because as far as you are concerned, "It is done!" This forms the basis of the "It is done!" method which we're going to talk about in the second half of this book.

Your higher self always knows what is best for you. It is the larger part of you that is always connected to the Universal Source, and knows your broader intentions and feelings perfectly. Similar teachings may refer to this as your subconscious, unconscious, higher consciousness, inner CEO, or the spirit or divine in you. The name by which you call it does not matter. The moment you set a conscious intention, your higher self works to deliver it to you. Perhaps more appropriately phrased from the earlier example: even if you do not set any conscious intention, your higher self is still trying to deliver greater good into your life. Therefore, it will try all ways and means to get through to you, to produce favorable conditions in your life. The only way to shut yourself off from this greater good is to constantly worry and think negative thoughts, or vibrate at a very negative level, which literally keeps your good from coming to you.

If I look back at my life, I can say that change started to happen for me when I actively engaged this greater part of myself. I shared this experience briefly in a chapter of my book "Banned Manifestation Secrets" which many readers have resonated with, and I think it warrants a more detailed retelling here so that you can understand how I came to these realizations.

Back in those days, I was still struggling with all of these Universal principles and wondering why they did not work in my life. As you know by now, the problem was my incessant worrying, a trait I inherited from my mother! However, this blockage was not obvious to me. At the same time, I started using some binaural sound tracks to improve my intuition. I reasoned—logically at that time—that if I could improve my intuition, I could perhaps find a way to "manifest" the things I wanted in my life.

Well, things did not turn out exactly the way I envisioned. Remember that the Universe always has higher and better plans for us. Instead, things turned out even *better* than I had envisioned! Within a short period of listening to the binaural soundtracks, a book title started popping into my head. This was a strange occurrence for me, as it had never happened before. In fact, I did not even know it was a book title until after I checked it out on Amazon! But this string of words started popping into my conscious awareness at around the same time I was listening to the binaural tapes, and they were: "How To Stop Worrying and Start Living." If you do a search on Amazon.com, you'll find that it is the title

RICHARD DOTTS

of a best-selling book by the great Dale Carnegie, who also wrote the classic "How To Win Friends & Influence People."

While I tell this story in my own bestselling book "Banned Manifestation Secrets," I did not reveal the book title I had received (which led to a string of emails from curious readers). Hopefully now the curiosity can be put to rest! What I am trying to convey here is **not** the fact that you will suddenly receive book titles out of the blue, or that you should listen to binaural beats like I did. Everyone's path is different, and the way something unfolds for you will be different from everyone else. Therefore, it is not usually useful to directly emulate or "copy" someone else's path. What you can do however, is to see how these principles can be applied—perhaps in a slightly different way—in your own life. (If you feel inspired to check it out, the binaural beats that I use and recommend for boosting intuition are from Immrama Institute. More information available at www.BannedManifestationSecrets.com/intuition)

The Universe Always Knows the Best Way to Reach You
I believe the Universe (my own higher self) was sending that title to me because it **already knew** what the cause of my blockage was. The cause of my problem of not being able to manifest desired results in my life was due to excessive *worrying*, and this was the Universe's way of getting through to me. The Universe will have other ways to get through to you. It may or may not be a book title, and you may

24

even receive a more direct revelation! I often joke that a book title was given to me because I love to read, and it was the most harmonious way in which the message could have received my attention. On the other hand, I am not a fan of movies (I watch perhaps one movie per year) and had a movie title been given to me instead—I would have missed out on the cue completely!

Fortunately, I acted on that Universal cue and purchased the book immediately, then read it. I also mentioned in "Banned Manifestation Secrets" that had I walked past this book on my own at the bookstore, I would have ignored it completely! This is because to my conscious, reasoning self, I had absolutely no idea that the root cause of my problem was worrying. I would not have put two and two together and connected the dots between my lack of manifestation results and my incessant worrying. And yet, the Universe knew this all along and got through to me at just the right opportune moment.

Did things change overnight after I started reading the book? I would love to say it was a drastic change, but really, the changes happened gradually. As I started to read the book (it was a thick book), I began to see the folly of worrying, and gradually that part of me started to fall away. It is interesting to note that the book does not talk about manifestations at all. It is not mentioned anywhere in the book that it will help you with your manifestations, or that it will help you in applying the Law of Attraction. The book was written long before the current self-help movement, and was supposed to be a pragmatic book for working professionals. Yet the message was just what I needed. It contained the right (and last) piece of the puzzle for me. Over the next few weeks and months, I read and re-read the book. I even purchased the audiobook version so I could listen to it in the car. The book inspired and moved me greatly—so much so that I was in tears at several points while listening to the audio version of the book. As a result, something within me shifted so fundamentally that it allowed me to live these techniques beautifully, as we are meant to.

So once again, I have to reiterate that in describing these experiences, I am using various aspects of my own experience to illustrate certain Universal Laws and principles. Things may **not** happen in the same way for you. Instead, they may happen in an even better and more beautiful way that is unique and just right for you! Therefore, it is important to remain open to all possibilities, for you never know how the Universe can deliver something to you. It may only be after the fact that you realize you have been given a truly precious gift from your higher self.

As I started practicing the techniques in the book in order to deal with my worries, I found that manifestations happened consistently. Things which I wanted so badly for the past few years started happening spontaneously, often with very little effort on my part. Things started moving along with a newfound sense of speed and momentum. At the beginning, I still could not connect the dots, but it was only after experiencing all the fascinating results that I finally saw a direct linkage between my level of negative thoughts and the results in my life. I had finally come full circle, into the desired life I have always been looking for, and it is now my intention to teach exactly the same principles to you.

Chapter Four
The Tale of Two Students

Throughout my life, I have freely shared these manifestation principles and techniques with various individuals who have asked me about them. Some of those with whom I've shared these techniques took to them immediately, and started creating changes very quickly in their own lives. Others struggled with these techniques and tried hard to apply them in their lives, but were frustrated with a lack of results. I estimate that out of all the people I have shared it with on a one-to-one basis over the years, only a handful of them really got it, while the remaining gave up and never tried again after a few initial failures.

Because I've had the luxury of interacting with the people I've shared these techniques with, I have gained an intimate, first-hand understanding as to why these techniques may work so beautifully for some, and yet provide no results for others. Sometimes, the process of helping others understand these techniques has brought me to a new level of clarity, revealing new insights for myself.

This is something I am always appreciative of. I often tell others that there isn't really a comprehensive book of "Universal principles" we can just find in the library and instantly gain access to all this esoteric knowledge. Because Universal Laws and principles are not easily observable, the application of these techniques certainly requires some clarification, especially for a new student.

The most notable example of someone who has successfully applied these techniques within a short time is that of my friend Mark. Within a short time of learning these techniques, Mark managed to double his monthly income, to a five-figure sum. He did this through reading my first book, "Banned Mind Control Secrets," and by directly clarifying some of the finer points with me. Within three months, he also had many miraculous manifestations happen for him in his life, such as his immediate family members winning top prizes in the lottery (twice!), and other serendipitous manifestations. I am recounting Mark's story briefly here to illustrate a point. First, the Universe does not care how long you have been studying these principles for. It does not reward "hard work." Instead, all the Universe cares about is whether you have done the required *inner* work to achieve an inner state of mind conducive to manifestations. This is also the reason why there truly is **no delay** between the time you set an intention for something, and the time it manifests in your life. If you are able to let go of all your resistance, fears and worries, then results will occur instantly for you—as quickly as you can allow them! This was certainly the case for my good friend, Mark. In his case, he did not have to go through a long period of studying and clarification like I did. While I read over 100 books a year on this subject and constantly try to improve my understanding of these Universal Laws, Mark was able to bring himself to a completely trusting inner state and to focus so strongly on his desires to the exclusion of everything else, that things happened really quickly for him. Therefore, manifestations are not conditional on how much you know, or how badly you want something. The sole criterion used by the Universe is whether you are in alignment or not. Any time you worry about when or how something is coming to you, you're out of alignment.

The first reason why things happened so quickly for my friend Mark is that he has a cheery and optimistic personality. He is an individual who is sporting and adventurous, and never shies away from trying new things in life. Therefore, when I suggested a series of manifestation exercises and practices for him to follow, he took to them immediately and started following my instructions without objection. On the other hand, some of the other friends I've worked with tended to be a little more skeptical. They wanted to know *why* we did something, or *how* it could help them—before they were willing to do it. While it helps to achieve a particular level of intellectual understanding, no amount of reasoning can substitute for the actual experience. For example, I have always read (and even intellectually accepted) that worrying is not conducive to manifestations occurring in our lives. Yet I still found a way to rationalize it because I had never *experienced* or lived this principle for myself. My understanding of it was based on a textbook—theoretical understanding.

The second reason why things happened quickly for Mark is the way he dealt with his own resistance, worries and fears. Any new student of these creative principles will certainly experience moments of fear and self-doubt. They are absolutely normal and to be expected! However, **how** you handle these fears, worries, and self-doubt makes a huge difference in your results. Do you allow them to run wild and completely overrule you? Or do you manage your worries and put them aside just for a moment? In the case of my friend Mark, he handled his initial lack of faith (in these principles) by placing his trust in me, and by observing me. He could see from my life that I was indeed living these principles, and the thought that someone had successfully applied these principles gave him the confidence he needed. Therefore, that was the special way in which Mark dealt with his initial fears and doubts. You can do the same too. In my early days of studying this material, I had no one in my immediate circle of friends to turn to. I didn't dare speak about the fact that I was interested in manifestation and these related subjects! Therefore, I kept my faith by reading books about this subject, and by drawing inspiration from the teachers who were successfully living these principles. It is advisable to find a close friend who is completely in agreement with you on this matter, and to practice these spiritual creative techniques together. Bear in mind that both of you have to make a one hundred percent commitment to putting these principles into action, to share success stories with one another and to encourage each other in times of doubt. It can be difficult to find a partner or mentor who may do this with you. As I write this, I have yet to find someone (apart from Mark, whom I can freely share this material with), but your creative journey *will* be fruitful if you can find a partner to do this work with.

The third most important point is that Mark followed my instructions to keep this work away from other people. No one else has to know that you are doing the work **except you**. He did not tell anyone, including his partner! It is not necessary to tell anyone else—so resist the urge to do so. It can be tempting at times to tell your family or friends about your manifestations or success stories, but that is seldom a good idea! Most people do not have an understanding of these Universal Laws, and telling them about your manifestations may stir up unwanted emotions or feelings within them. Furthermore, they may try to convince you that it is just a "coincidence", and that things would have happened anyway. This is the number one excuse which new students often use to rationalize their early successes. They often say, "It would have happened anyway!" Once you start falling into this "it would have happened anyway" trap, you'll lose the much-needed faith in the process. When Mark had a string of successes in the beginning, I constantly encouraged him and told him that they were the direct result of these new techniques he was applying in his life. Since we frequently discussed this material, I could help him understand that none of these good things had happened to him in his life *until* he set conscious intentions and started practicing these techniques. Therefore, it helped him strengthen his faith and belief in these Universal principles.

Even for a seasoned practitioner of the material like me, there were times when I felt tempted to dismiss certain events in my life as mere coincidences. But then I took a closer look at my life and observed when certain events happened. For example, take the fact that I received a phone call from an old client right out of the blue—just two weeks after I set a conscious intention to increase my income. These incidents make me realize that nothing in life happens by accident, and that everything happens in direct response to our thoughts and feelings in every moment.

Having discussed the case of a successful student of this material, let's now talk about another friend of mine who did not have success applying this same material. In both cases, I taught the exact same material to both parties. Let's call him J. The truth is that there is a bit of J in everyone. Everyone has their own periods of fear and self-doubt—even me—which can stretch over a period of a few years. I write about these experiences in my book "What to Do When You Are Stuck." That was the period in my life when I was reading self-help book after self-help book—to no avail. I felt that nothing was flowing into my life, and nothing I tried seemed to work. I realize today that I am exactly the same person I was back then, except that I have a completely new perspective on things now. My mindset has changed. My inner state has changed, and as a result, my outer reality is completely different.

J was also very interested in these manifestation techniques, and he wanted to use them to manifest a new car and more money. However, J was also very skeptical and deeply rooted in reason. Deep down inside, he could not believe that he could get "something for nothing." He operated with a sense of distrust about the world and with other people. He wanted to see the path through which something could happen for him. Therefore, when he asked for a new car, he wanted to see how the car would come to him, or how he could somehow earn enough money to buy the car. Wanting to know the *how* is a recipe for disappointment—because if you know all the *hows*, you would have done it already, and there would be no need to ask the Universe at all! Another recipe for disappointment is to specify **how** something should come to you, without really believing that it is possible. For example, J wanted to buy a very expensive sports car, and the "how" he specified was that he would earn a certain amount of money needed to buy that car. However, he had not yet convinced himself that it was possible to earn that amount of money, therefore, he had two trust issues to deal with—first, whether to trust that these Universal Laws could work and second, whether to trust that he could indeed earn that kind of money!

You can see clearly from this example, how we set up self-imposed limitations for ourselves. By consistently focusing on the fact that he needed that particular sum of money and the fact that he did not have it, J was in fact reinforcing his existing, *stuck* reality. On the other hand, Mark sidestepped the same issues by cleverly "thinking around" them. First, he trusted the Universal Laws by observing that they had worked for me. Since I am a trusted friend of his, it increased his trust in the Universal Laws. Second, Mark's naturally trusting disposition led him to drop all his unwanted resistance around his desired manifestations very quickly.

You can therefore look at instant manifestations as being comprised of two aspects: First, the individual must completely give up the need to worry over how something will come to him. He must give up any fear of not having the thing he wants. The moment you do so and let go of your fear, things will happen very quickly for you, in unimaginable ways. Second, an individual must be willing to embrace the unknown and the unseen spiritual forces that are constantly working around them. By this, I mean giving up the *hows* and just accepting that which you are asking for is being delivered to you through the best and most harmonious way possible, this very moment. It is done! You must give up the desire to meddle in *how* something will come to you, and accept that if you do your part of the work, the Universe will do its part. In the next chapter, I'll talk about the biggest "unseen" hurdles that prevent manifestations, and how you can gently bring them into your awareness.

CHAPTER FIVE

UNSEEN BLOCKS THAT DELAY YOUR MANIFESTATIONS

There are two kinds of blocks that delay your manifestations. The first kind is specific, and the second kind is more general. To be an effective creator and manifestor, you need to eliminate both types of blocks from your life. When I use the word "block," I am generally referring to resistance; unwanted feelings or thoughts that block your manifestations. Anything that delays or blocks your good from coming to you is considered a hurdle.

As I've spent the first four chapters of this book explaining, a good many of these blocks are so pervasive that you probably cannot see them at first. It is also very likely that you will argue against their existence, or convince yourself that they do not apply in your case. However, when the urge to do so comes up, look at the results in a particular area in your life. The results never lie. Are you getting the desired results you want in a certain area of your life? If you are being blocked in a particular area, chances are that you are thinking lackful thoughts or blocking your own progress in that area. Therefore, it would help if you use the techniques in this chapter to directly address these blocks. Everyone has the ability to create and manifest, without exception. However, those who are effective creators and manifestors have found ways to dissolve these blocks in such a way that their manifestative powers can shine through.

Dealing with General "Something Will Go Wrong" Fears

The first type of block I'll discuss here is general fear. This means wide, all-encompassing fear that many of us feel from time to time. For example, the feeling that something is about to "go wrong," even (or especially) when nothing is happening at all. These spontaneous worries are the result of long periods of negative conditioning we have received, causing us to automatically worry that something is wrong when things go too well for us.

Many of us have been taught to "be ready for disaster" or to pre-empt problems, which results in us thinking that something bad is about to happen—especially when things appear all smooth and rosy! This block is very subtle and pervasive, and it can indeed be difficult to pinpoint in the beginning. Therefore, you can be right in the middle of it and not even realize it! I remember falling into this trap during my early days, when I thought that life was supposed to be a series of problems. You can imagine that I was often on the lookout for potential problems to prevent or solve—and I found a lot of them in those days! Nowadays, I believe that life is a series of magical and miraculous moments, where good things happen to us frequently—and it's what I find most of the time. I'm still the same person on the outside, but my inner state has changed so completely that those around me have picked up on this complete change.

The first step in dissolving this block is to gently bring it into your awareness. Ask yourself whether you sometimes worry when things are going too well, or whether you secretly wonder when things are going to finally go wrong. Catch yourself when you have such thoughts and examine them. You'll realize that these worry- or fear-thoughts are completely illogical, and are grounded in past fears instead of solid facts.

Why should things going well be an indication of problems to come? That's certainly an illogical assumption, and one rooted in the belief that we are "not good enough" or "not deserving enough" for all of this good in our lives. The way to turn this self-sabotaging form of thinking around is easy. Each time you catch yourself wondering when the good times will end, or when something bad will happen, gently acknowledge the thought and **reverse** it. **Tell yourself that the opposite is just as true**: "More good things can happen to me at any time." Or, "I can't wait to receive the good that is on its way to me!" or "There is no limit to the good that I can experience!" This immediately releases the worry-thoughts without you engaging in them at all. Focus on doing this each time general fear-thoughts crop up, and you'll soon find that they don't occur as frequently for you, because you have gently let them go.

How to Deal with an Incessant Need to Worry

Now that we have dealt with this general fear of things going wrong, let's discuss more specific emotions and negative feelings that can delay your manifestations. The first, which we have spent much of this book discussing, is that of worrying. I've explained that worrying affects your manifestations because it causes you to dwell on and spend lots of time on thinking about unwanted outcomes.

Worry is essentially the act of thinking about various ways things can go wrong, and conjuring up images of various unwanted outcomes in our minds. When we worry, our imaginations often go into overdrive, and as a result, we vividly feel the negative emotions and feelings that go along with the unwanted scenarios we are worrying about. Realize that worrying is actually a very effective visualization session—just that it is a form of *negative* visualization. You are literally using all of your creative energies and putting them into creating an outcome which you do not want! Therefore, nothing good can ever come out of worrying, and I encourage you to set an intention to drop the habit immediately. Realizing that worrying is an effective form of visualization will probably do the trick for most people. It certainly did the trick for me!

When it comes to curbing the habit of worrying, recognize that worrying about anything is futile. Reading "How to Stop Worrying and Start Living" by Dale Carnegie, the book title that was given to me, can be immensely helpful.

But here are a few general rules of thumb. First, if you can do anything to change the outcome, you should be taking active steps towards changing the outcome instead of spending time worrying about possible doomsday scenarios. In other words, your time can be much better spent taking steps to solve the problem. Second, if the outcome cannot be changed through any action on your part, no amount of worrying is going to help. In that case, why even worry at all? In situations like this, when it is not up to you, affirm and visualize a positive outcome, dwell on it frequently and leave everything to the Universe.

A person who worries is someone who does not yet fully comprehend the powerful creative laws of the Universe. He or she does not yet know the powerful creative faculties we have at our disposal to create any reality which we desire. If we truly know how powerful we are as creative beings, we would spend no time at all worrying, and all our time focused on creating our desired outcomes, by tapping into these Universal Laws using our mental faculties. I am reminded of a beautiful quote from Abraham-Hicks: "Fear only exists when you do not understand that you have the power to project thought and that the Universe will respond." Wow! What a powerful statement that is! We are afraid when we see ourselves as powerless victims. But that fear completely dissipates when we step into our roles as powerful creators. The "It is done" technique that I'll share will be very useful for doing so.

How Do I Know if I'm Doing These Steps Correctly?
Sometimes, we also worry over whether these Universal principles will work, or whether we are doing them correctly. New students of this material often ask me, "How do I know if I am doing the steps correctly as intended?" Spiritual teachers often answer that there *is no right way* to do any of this, and that there is no way to get anything wrong! Indeed, I often teach that the only way you can get it "wrong" is not to do anything at all—and the "right" way is that whichever works for you.

Don't take any of the steps I (or any other spiritual teacher) have written as being cast in stone. The broader principles are there to guide you, but the finer steps on how to do it are completely up to you. For example, when we tell you to eliminate worry from your life and stop worrying about things, that's a broader Universal principle. How you apply this principle is up to you, and whichever method you can find to free yourself from the tentacles of worrying will be just as useful for you.

Now let's deal with the issue of worrying over whether these manifestation principles will work. Students often worry about whether these principles will work, and whether something they have asked for will come to them. This is somewhat related to having a distrust in these Universal principles. This distrust is natural in the beginning. Amongst everyone I have worked with, only a very small percentage of them (my friend, Mark, being one of them) have been able to completely trust in their application of this material. The remaining had many doubts, and even suspicions as to whether all of these will work for them. Therefore, another major block which we have to deal with while applying these Universal Laws is the issue of trust.

Again, distrust is the result of long periods of negative conditioning, where we have been taught not to be so trusting of others, and to be wary of things that appear "too good to be true." Realize that this way of functioning in the world stems from lackful or limited thinking along these lines: "There is not enough to go around, therefore I have to guard whatever I have very carefully in case someone takes it away from me." I can't help but think back to the perfect example of a newborn baby, who just trusts that everyone will take good care of it and all its needs will be met. As a result, Universal force often acts *through* those around the baby to ensure that this is so.

Have you ever observed how the parents and those around a baby are willing to do anything for the baby, even if it means laying down their own lives to protect the infant in times of danger? There is a powerful, Universal force that compels us to act in this manner—this is the divine that flows through us. The same force that brings all of your good to you, orchestrates and organizes every single little detail in the Universe. If it can happen for the little baby, why can't it happen for the rest of us? Begin to trust in these Universal Laws a little more, one bit at a time. Observing how a baby is so trusting and peaceful is often a good spiritual exercise. The next time you are around a baby, observe how Universal forces rally all the adults around the baby to provide for it. You will even feel a sudden, gentle impulse to cuddle, love and protect the baby yourself! You may call this instinct or behavior that is hard-wired, but it is really our fundamental Universal forces at work. These forces are powerful, and are the same forces that will bring your manifestations to you.

People often tell me that we live in a danger-ous world, and that we should not be so trusting of others. Since placing my complete trust in these Universal Laws, no harm has befallen me, because my consciousness simply does not allow such a pos-sibility. I do not even dwell—on a moment, or on the possibility of anything bad or untoward happening to me. As a result, I am safe, happy and well-protected at all times in my life. People who are distrustful often believe that others are out to harm them in some way or another, or that they have to protect themselves from external dangers. As a result, what do you think their consciousness is mostly focused on? That's right, dangers and unwanted outcomes. Therefore, be careful about what you are actually attracting more of into your life. You may think that you want to stay safe and protected, when in actual fact your focus may be on just the opposite—the things that you do not want to have happen to you.

If you find it difficult to place your faith and trust in these Universal Laws for now, an easier way would be to find a teacher you believe in and place your faith and trust in him or her. You do not need to communicate with the teacher personally. I've known many great teachers just from reading their books. For many, it can be easier to place their faith in a single person. I can assure you that since I've adopted a totally trusting mindset, nothing bad or untoward has happened to me. Instead, my life has blossomed to even greater levels and I find myself divinely provided for and protected in the most amazing of circumstances! Sometimes I look back and realize that something "bad" could have happened to me, but I just side-stepped the issue completely through divine timing. Once again, if your vibrations are nowhere near those of negative events and circumstances, then negative events and circumstances have no way of happening to you— no matter how "physically" near them you may be. Therefore, the choice of which reality you wish to participate in at any moment is always up to you.

Due to our education process, we often complicate matters needlessly. For example, the number one objection people often have is: "It can't be this simple! Life can't be as simple as just asking for what we want. If it is so, everyone will be successful!" This is a very common objection that prevents them from even *trying* out these principles and teachings. If you really think about it, this line of reasoning is absurd, because what they are saying is that if something is simple, it cannot possibly work, and therefore they are not trying it.

My answer is always the same—how can you be so sure? Some of the most profound things in life are also the simplest. There is nothing complicated in nature, just as there is nothing complicated in life. The Universe always seeks to deliver our good to us in the most straightforward and harmonious ways possible. Nature always takes the path of least resistance. Observe a plant growing and you'll find that it does so through the path of least resistance, going around any obstacle. It does not try to stubbornly break through the obstacle if there is an easier path. The same goes for your body, and other natural phenomena. So why the need to complicate matters and make things more difficult than they appear? I find that the answer once again boils down to the conditioning we have received. We often want to appear as sophisticated as possible to others, so that we come across as intelligent. We take pride in doing things that others can't. Therefore, people and companies often complicate things to try and sell us more solutions. We assume that people will not want to pay a lot of money for simple solutions, and therefore complex solutions are often sold to us at high prices, with a lot of bells and whistles involved.

When it comes to these Universal Laws, I can assure you that there is absolutely nothing complicated about their application. Life is meant to be simple, and this is the way you were meant to live and function. You are meant to be a creative being, endowed with creative abilities to make things happen at will. You are not meant to spent most of your time moving against the grain and struggling to get things done. The struggle is always optional, unless you choose it as part of your experience.

I have observed a return to simplicity and ease, time and time again in my life, and in the lives of many others in our society. At a time when our lives become more complex, our old models and paradigms often break down, necessitating that we move to a whole new level of understanding and simplicity. The new models are not more complex than the old ones; instead, they are simpler and less complicated, because we have learned how to discard the unwanted components from our older, outdated models and simply focus on the things that are absolutely necessary. Therefore, a return to simplicity is always at the core of our being.

Universal Laws are not complicated. They are not difficult. The truth is always simple. Give up the notion that you have to go through a complicated process just because you are asking for something "big." Again, I often mention that all separation is at the level of the ego, and that the Universe does not discriminate between "big" or "small" requests. The same Universal principles apply to each and every one of them.

CHAPTER SIX

THE UNIVERSE HAS NO ULTERIOR MOTIVE

Perhaps the hardest thing for me to "get" in my early days of learning these principles was dealing with the inner, nagging questions that constantly popped up at the back of my head:

What is the catch?
Why does everything sound so simple and easy?
Is that all I have to do?
Why is the Universe so kind?

I recognize today that these questions arose from my lackful and limited thinking, and were a direct reflection of the negative conditioning I had received all my life. The questions we spontaneously ask reflect our levels of consciousness. This is the same when learning any new subject. As a teacher of various subjects, I observe in my classes that a beginning student tends to ask beginner questions that a more advanced student may find silly or stupid. But do not dismiss these "beginner" questions, for they are absolutely essential in the learning process. Instead, see them as the stepping stones that they are. These questions are there to help and guide you toward higher levels of consciousness. They reveal the fallacies in our understanding, which can then be corrected. Looking at the questions we ask ourselves throughout the day gives us an idea of our current level of consciousness: A fearful person is constantly asking fear-based questions. The lackful individual is constantly asking lack-based questions (e.g. How do I get enough?), and the abundant individual is always asking abundant questions (e.g. Why am I so rich and how can I put it to good use?).

Anthony Robbins is famous for his saying that "the quality of your life depends on the quality of questions that you ask." This statement is certainly true. Questions focus our attention and move us in the direction we want to go. By asking a properly-phrased question, we direct our attention and focus to either wanted or unwanted outcomes. However, this saying also presupposes that we can change the questions we ask at will. In actual fact, the behind-the-scenes process is much more complicated than that. The questions that we ask reflect our existing levels of consciousness and belief, and changing the questions that we ask requires that we elevate our selves to higher levels of consciousness.

One question a new student of this material may have is: Are things really so simple? Does the Universe have an ulterior motive? Let's put this issue to rest once and for all. After years of being on the spiritual path, and trying out all these Universal principles for myself, I have come to realize that no, the Universe does not have any ulterior motive. There are no dark forces out there trying to coerce us into doing things we do not want to do, or into wanting certain "bad" things to happen to us. There are no beings out there trying to gain control over us. These concepts result from a misunderstanding of spiritual principles, which can cause unnecessary delays in the manifestation process.

Our egos and reasoning minds are meant to protect us and keep us safe. Therefore, when we try to give up control to the Universe or to let things happen by themselves without knowing the hows or the whys, you can be assured that the ego and our logical selves will kick up a huge ruckus. The ego will not be ready to let go without a strong fight, just as you have so strongly identified with your reasoning faculties throughout your lifetime. What you are doing now threatens its very existence! As such, when you first learn this material or try any manifestation techniques, your logical mind will attempt to persuade and convince you (oftentimes very convincingly) that all this is a bunch of hogwash, that it is too good to be true, or that if things were so simple, everyone would be millionaires already. If you believe this "logic" that your conscious, reasoning mind is trying to present to you, then you may never go back to trying these techniques again. Or you may try them once and then give up. Similarly, at every apparent "failure" or "lack of results" when you apply these techniques, your logical mind will jump at the opportunity to say "See, I told you so! There is no free lunch in this world!" Once again, if you believe in these thoughts, you will again be moving further and further away from your desired outcomes.

When you adopt a new level of spiritual understanding, such negative thoughts cease to be an issue in your mind. Notice that every problem, is really a problem first "in your mind." I am able to apply manifestation techniques very effectively today, because I have engaged the full cooperation of my unconscious self, in such a way that it does not unknowingly impede my progress. My unconscious self has stopped sending me worry, and fearful or distrustful thoughts. In their place, I have a deep and profound sense of peace and trust, which I will teach you how to achieve with a very effective "It is done" technique.

Therefore, when distrustful thoughts surface in your mind—see them for what they really are—as just a thought or a feeling. A thought can be changed at any time into a more resourceful one. It is not sufficient to just try these Universal principles and techniques on one hand while not believing in them. The key is to immerse yourself into an atmosphere of complete trust, even if it is just for a moment. If you find yourself distrustful, then allow yourself to trust just for a moment. Ask yourself whether you are able to give up your distrust "just for now." You can always go back to your logical, reasoning self afterwards.

But just for the next ten to fifteen minutes, allow yourself to completely trust in the dependability of these Universal Laws. Allow yourself to feel their power and the energy moving in your body as you state your intentions. I go into greater detail over how to do this in my book, "Playing in Time and Space," which offers a few effective techniques for moving yourself into new alternate realities conducive for manifestations to take place.

Another common block that can delay your manifestations is the feeling of impatience. You know what impatience feels like, when you keep asking yourself *when* something is going to be here, or *why* is it not here yet. It is that feeling you have when you set a deadline to receive something, or that desperate feeling that you must get something by a particular time or date.

Impatience is a very common feeling that ironically, delays our manifestations. The more desperately you want something, the further you hold it away from you—because first of all, your impatience stems from the acute recognition of the fact that you do not have what you desire yet! Therefore, the more impatient you get, the more energy you channel into the fact that something is not here yet—and the more you perpetuate your current *stuck* reality.

One of the common "mistakes" in dealing with impatience is to try and convince yourself that you are actually patient. You may try to stop thinking about a particular object or outcome, just to convince yourself that it does not really matter to you.

Or you may say the words, "Well, I am not impatient. I don't really care when it comes to me." However, know that the Universe responds not to your words but perfectly to your vibrational frequency, every single time. You cannot *feign* patience or even appear to be indifferent on the outside. You have to truly *feel* it on the inside. I know, because I once used all these ploys in an attempt to convince **myself** that I was not impatient, when in actual fact I was highly concerned over when my manifestations were appearing. I was at the point of desperation!

Know that because the Universe is picking up on everything so perfectly all of the time, that you cannot hide your true feelings from the Universe. Therefore, the only option left is to really let go of any impatience. Understanding the reasons behind your impatience can be a great help.

Why are we impatient in the first place? If you really examine the reasons for your impatience, it can boil down to the same few. First, we are impatient because we think something should be here by a particular date, and it has not arrived yet. In setting a deadline, we are imposing a "how" on the Universe. We are dictating "when" it should come to us. Know that everything always happens in its own perfect way, and in its own perfect time for the Universe. The Universe always knows our highest good, and the most harmonious way to deliver something to us. Therefore, how can you be so sure that the timeline you have dictated is what is "best" for you? You may think you need something—perhaps a certain sum of money urgently—but the Universe always has better plans for you. Maybe circumstances will change in such a way that you do not need that sum of money after all (as it has happened to me more than once), or that you may not even need money at all to get the thing done (as has also happened to me, again more than once).

These things have happened so frequently that I now completely give up any control of how something is going to happen in my life. I can't tell you how much unnecessary struggle I have dealt with, trying to dictate that the Universe deliver a particular sum of money to me at a particular date, in order to fulfil a particular need I have identified. But going into such great detail is doing things the hard way! I once visualized over and over again, that the Universe would deliver a sum of money to me so that I could make a particular trip. It turned out that circumstances changed and I did not even need to make the trip at all. So be very open to all possibilities. Anytime you are feeling impatient, ask yourself whether you are restricting your possibilities.

The second common reason for impatience leads back to two of our earlier blocks—fear and worry. We are impatient because we are secretly afraid that something will not happen for us, and therefore we want it to happen fast. **Read the previous sentence again and make sure that the meaning becomes entirely clear to you**. We are impatient because we do not trust in the process entirely. There is a part of us that secretly thinks nothing is going to happen, therefore we keep stating our intentions and doing all the processes to ensure that what we ask for does happen. Again, once you deal with the issues of distrust and fear (of something *not* coming to you), the impatience dissolves and falls away of its own accord. Therefore, the one pervasive block that you really need to deal with is worry.

The first step in dealing with all these blocks is to first **recognize** their existence. The moment you recognize their existence, you immediately dissolve much of their power over you because previously, you were operating under their unconscious influences. But now, your power of awareness makes it easier for you to sidestep them. Think back to the earlier story about my friend Mark, who picked up these manifestation techniques very quickly and easily, despite not having engaged in a long and intense study of this material. One main reason is because Mark started his journey without having to deal with the blocks of worry, impatience, distrust or fear. Whenever any of these feelings came up for him, he was able to handle them effectively because I had already forewarned him about them, and I had also told him to *expect* them.

Perhaps unfortunately, this is where many other manifestation books and techniques often fall short. They are so focused on the actual techniques, steps and processes that no adequate mention is given to the fact that you do need to remove the four major blocks of worry, impatience, distrust and fear before your manifestations start to appear. The converse is also true. The moment you properly deal with and release worry, impatience, distrust and fear from your life, then it does not matter what manifestation technique or process you use. In fact, you don't even have to ask much at all because then, good things that are aligned with your highest desires will start happening spontaneously in your life. Since the Universe always picks up on all your feelings and vibrations perfectly, doesn't it make perfect sense that it also picks up on your desires and delivers them to you in the smoothest way possible? But it can only do so if you give up your habits of worrying and feeling impatient, or feeling distrustful or fearful. Your manifestation success will be in direct proportion to your ability to give up these blocks.

Now that you have the basic understanding of how these four blocks can potentially delay your manifestations, I am going to guide you through the "It is done" process that deals with the four major blocks we discussed earlier, and also puts you in a highly conducive manifestation inner state.

Chapter Seven

The Significance of "It Is Done!"

Modern prayers in the Western world end with an "amen", which when loosely translated means, "and so it is" or "it is done." The "amen" one utters at the end of a prayer signifies that we have turned the problem completely over to God (or to the Universe), and that **nothing more needs to be done**. No more worrying over the outcome, no more fear, no more struggle or strife. It is done! Everything is already fulfilled and in a perfect state of harmonious completion.

I feel that in modern times however, we add "amen" at the end of our prayers more out of habit and convention, without really knowing the full significance of what this word means. The first time I read about the meaning of "amen," goosebumps ran all over my body as I finally understood the true significance of prayer. In the act of praying, you state your desire clearly. At the end of it, the utterance of "amen" is more than just a symbolic gesture. It is your display of complete faith and trust in these Universal Laws you are relying on. It is meant to signify that your faith is so deep, you consider what you have asked for complete and done. There is nothing more you have to do, and the perfect conditions which you hope for are already here.

I believe this was the intention of the ancient spiritual masters when they prayed in this fashion. A study of other spiritual traditions and religions shows that each tradition has its own way of ending a prayer, and it usually ends with the same affirmative word or phrase each time. Modern man seems to have glossed over this convention, placing more weight on the actual contents of the prayer and the words that are said—but what is actually of profound importance is what is said at the **end** of the prayer. More clearly stated, it is how you *feel* when you conclude your prayer.

I have chosen to substitute the word "amen" for something which is more easily understood and accessible in our daily English language. The short phrase I have chosen is, "It is done!" Try saying "It is done!" to yourself right now, and *feel* how good it feels. Bask in the good feeling of it! I can just close my eyes right now and imagine that wonderful "it is done!" feeling. Even saying it quietly to yourself gives you a sense of peace, closure, completion, satisfaction and fulfillment. Your mind and body know this feeling as the feeling of assurance, one of peace and complete satisfaction, resting in the awareness that everything has happened just according to how you intended it to.

Think back to a time in the past when you completed a task, any task, and then triumphantly told yourself, "It is done!" at the end of it. How did you feel at that moment? Did you feel at the top of the world? Did you feel invincible, powerful and completely fulfilled? You may even be feeling those feelings now as you think back to that wonderful moment. That feeling of deep peace, satisfaction and happiness is what we are looking for here. The "it is done" method brings this feeling into your daily life and your daily manifestation practice such that you bring yourself to an inner state that is extremely conducive for manifestations to take place.

The more you use this "it is done!" technique, the more it will work for you. This is because you will be anchoring and deepening this inner state each time you repeat the technique. With each success, you'll have more "it is done" moments to draw upon—so the process literally compounds itself each and every time you use it! It is certainly not an exaggeration or understatement to say that the "it is done" technique gets better and more powerful over time. There is both scientific and spiritual evidence to back this up, and very soon you'll find that the "it is done" technique helps to erase any negativity or worries in your life just like that—with no fuss.

Let me first share with you the significance of "it is done." I have chosen these three English words to represent this inner state and inner feeling. However, understand that I'm talking about something that goes beyond mere words. I am simply using these three words, as the ancient spiritual masters used "amen," to signify the perfect completion and fruition of something. If you treat "it is done" as just another phrase, word, or utterance, then it is going to be just that for you. Just three words strung together. However, know that it is **not** just another phrase or three simple words. These are three very powerful words that have the power to instantly bring you into another world, right into an inner state that is conducive to manifestations.

At the beginning, you may need to say these three words either out loud or quietly to yourself. However, as you become more familiar with this practice, you'll find (as many have) that **no words are necessary**. How is that even possible? Remember that these words are merely a bridge, a conduit—to a magical inner state. Therefore by saying them, you are invoking and accessing this inner state of possibilities within yourself. Once you are accustomed to how the "it is done" state of being feels, you do not even have to say the words to get there. You can get there at will. You can get there no matter what you are doing, or where you are.

In the beginning, it may be necessary for you to close your eyes in order to shut out any distractions and really be attuned to your inner feelings. However, I encourage that as you gradually practice this technique, that you do it with your eyes open.

Also do it in a variety of situations. Initially, it may only be possible to practice this technique when you are alone in a quiet place. However, as time passes, you may find that you can do this anywhere, even in moments of stress and perceived crisis. You can move into the "it is done" inner state anytime and anywhere, and your physical location or surroundings simply will not matter.

What does the "it is done" inner state feel like? The earlier example in which we thought about the successful completion of a project, or the successful resolution of a problem comes close enough. However, each situation is different, and you must use your imagination somewhat to bring yourself into the "it is done" feeling. A question I like to ask to guide myself is this: how would I feel, if it is done? How would I feel if I get what I'm asking for? How would I feel if this issue is resolved? That is the "it is done" feeling you are going for.

Remember that you can feel this feeling at any time, independent of outer circumstances or reality. There is no condition or clause anywhere that states that you can *only* feel the feeling of completion when physical reality matches up. Since you are imbued with the powers of a creator, you are able to choose your own thoughts and *feel* anything you want at any time, **independent of** outer circumstances! While this may seem like a trivial point, know that it is actually very profound because it means that **you have a choice, in every moment.**

You can use this "it is done" technique during moments of crises or apparent problems. I sometimes use it for these unexpected circumstances, and it helps calm me down very quickly. Because I have used this technique so many times and repeated this phrase so many times, I am actually drawing on the collective power of all my past successes when I use this technique. I am drawing on the thousands of times that the technique has worked for me and applying that power to the new situation. When you have the benefit of tapping into your past successes, you'll find that any blocks you have instantly melt away. You'll find your fears, worries, impatience and distrust melt away with the use of this technique.

When you use the "it is done" technique, you have to **really mean it**. You cannot just append it to the end of an intention, affirmation or statement as an afterthought. Doing so would be falling into the trap that millions make when they say "amen" after their prayers. They treat "amen" as nothing more than an afterthought, instead of seeing the phrase for what it really is. I would argue that "it is done" is actually more important than the actual intention itself, because what you are doing is taking that intention and directly imprinting the collective energy field with the signature vibrational patterns of your intention. I still have no clear explanation of how the process works, but I know that it just works. This method cuts through the four major blocks that I discussed earlier.

Before we go into discussing this technique in detail, let me tell you about an experience I had with using the technique recently. I use all these techniques and methods I teach on a regular basis, because they have been distilled after a long period of learning these spiritual laws and Universal Principles. I use and teach only what works. Recently I was in a meditation session, and I had the intention to win a prize at a lucky draw. This lucky draw is a bit special; it is organized by a shopping mall in which a certain amount of money spent allows you one chance at a "jackpot machine." I have played this game well over ten times in the past few years and have not won anything. However, I thought it would be nice if I could actually win something, so I visualized myself playing the "jackpot" machine, seeing the notification on screen that I had won a prize, and actually queuing up to collect my prize.

Your usual visualization would entail similar steps: seeing the desired outcome in your mind, and feeling the feelings associated with your desired outcome as vividly as possible. However, there is one additional step in the "it is done" process, and **it is key.** The "it is done" technique serves to reinforce and deeply imprint the intentions you have stated, and the feelings you have felt during the previous visualization process. At the conclusion of the visualization or statement, what you do is to mentally say "it is done" to yourself—and at the same time **feel** the totality of the feelings associated with this phrase. How would you feel if **it is done?** Feel this feeling in the moment of saying this phrase quietly to yourself. "It" refers to whatever you have asked for earlier, so the Universe already knows perfectly what you are referring to. There is no need to repeat or visualize the whole outcome again. Instead, just focus on feeling the "it is done" feeling. As you say the statement, feel yourself moving powerfully into a state of completion. I always feel goosebumps all over my body and the movement of energy around and through me. You will feel the same thing, too.

After you have allowed yourself to move into this powerful state, stay still and silent for a moment, with your eyes closed if necessary. Feel the completion that has just taken place. Whatever you have asked for **is already here and fulfilled.** There is nothing more you need to do or have to do.

I added this "it is done" process to my earlier visualization. I knew in that moment there was nothing more I needed to do, so off I went for an enjoyable dinner with my family. After dinner, I joined the queue to play one of the "jackpot" machines—and exactly as I had visualized, I won an instant prize! Now know that in my past three years of joining this little draw, I had never won anything. Each time I played, I saw other shoppers leaving empty-handed as well. However, this time was different. I joined the queue to collect my prize just as I had envisioned.

I did not engage in a highly detailed visualization session. In fact, I did not even know what words would appear on the screen to inform me that I had won, or the physical placement of the machines and the queue. So I merely made all of that up in my visualization based on whatever I could recall from memory. Those are not as important as the *feelings*, which make up your inner state. Remember that as Neville puts it, "feeling is the secret" and nothing is more important than that "it is done" feeling. What I did when I added the "it is done" process to the end, was to display my faith and trust in the Universe that it was indeed done, and that in that very moment, my prize was already reserved for me. I did not worry about *whether* it would happen, or how it would come to me. I was very calm and relaxed about the whole affair.

You'll also notice that I did not have a particularly good reason for wanting to win a prize. There are some books which teach that you need to have a burning desire, or a compelling, good reason for wanting something. I have found that having a good reason usually aids in the visualization process, which in turn allows you to add more vivid feelings to the process. However, don't be afraid to ask for something just for the sake of wanting it! Sometimes, that can be the purest of intentions.

I wanted to win a prize because I had never won before, and I wanted to experience the thrill of winning. My intention was pure and simple. I simply wanted to give myself the fun **experience** of queuing up to collect my prize, and it happened! Therefore, I would not encourage that you start writing or even listing a long list of reasons for why you *should* have something, or why you deserve something. Those are not important to the Universe. Pay very close attention to how you feel when you do an exercise of listing down the reasons for why you should have something—part of you wants the thing badly, and another part of you feels that you probably do not deserve it, which is why the long list of reasons are necessary to convince yourself of your worthiness in the first place.

Know that the Universe always delivers to you whatever you ask for, without judgment, and there is no need to "prove" your deservingness or worthiness in any way. You can want something simply just for the sake of wanting it, because your wanting of something does not deprive another from his or her share! You are already worthy of all the good there is, and if something does not come to you, it is not because you're not asking hard enough—but because you are unknowingly blocking it from coming to you. The "it is done" technique will help you quickly get past these blocks.

Chapter Eight

The "It Is Done" Process in Detail

The beauty of the "it is done" technique is that it is compatible with any spiritual practice that you are currently doing. No matter what technique of meditation, creative visualization or creative process you are using, the "it is done" technique does not require you to change any of it one bit. You can continue to use what has worked for you in the past. Instead, the "it is done" technique offers a powerful add-on that complements whatever technique or process you are currently using. As you use the "it is done" technique on a consistent basis, you'll not only tap into the power of all your past intentions that have successfully manifested, but you'll also be able to access these powerful emotions and feelings at will.

How to Apply the "It Is Done!" Technique

I am now going to share the first method of using the "it is done" technique, which is at the end of any manifestation process you may already be doing. No

matter what visualization or intention-stating process you are using, simply append the "it is done"
process to the end of it. You may choose to say the
words out loud, or say them to yourself (as I prefer
to do). This is how I usually practice the "it is done"
technique:

1. Find a quiet spot or place where you will not
    be disturbed for the next five to ten minutes.
    Initially, it helps to find a private spot where you
    can do this exercise without any fear of being
    interrupted. Make sure that the spot is just right
    and comfortable for you, and remove any dis-
    tractions from the area.

2. Close your eyes and take three deep breaths.
    Breathe in deep and feel the energy flowing all
    over your body. Feel the good feelings and sensa-
    tions as you inhale deeply.

3. Breathe out slowly, and with each exhalation,
    feel yourself becoming more and more relaxed.
    Know that you are becoming more and more
    relaxed.

4. After taking three deep breaths, proceed to visu-
    alize your desire or state your intention. (At this
    point, you can do whatever manifestation prac-
    tice you usually do. I will describe my practice
    in the next few sentences.) As you do so, form

a mental picture in your mind about the desire already fulfilled. For example, I saw myself queuing up to collect my prize after I played the game. I also felt the elation and happy emotions as I was queuing up to collect my prize. Take as much time as necessary at this step so that you can feel the emotions clearly. As you do so, tell yourself that it is happening not in the future, but **right now**. Feel your desires coming true and happening for you **right now**, at this very moment, and not at some spot out there in the future.

5. When you have visualized everything to your satisfaction or you have stated your intentions to your satisfaction, say "It is done!" silently to yourself and feel the "it is done" feelings peaking. I find it useful to repeat the phrase three times consecutively, saying it out loud in my mind firmly, as a proclamation.

Now, this is important—do not just go through the motions and add the words "it is done" to the end of your manifestation process. Know that the magic is actually happening when you say "It is done!" When you say the phrase to yourself silently, you are doing nothing less than moving energy. You are literally shaping the energy field and imprinting it with your own intentions! Therefore, proclaim the three words to yourself and **really feel them. Really**

feel the meaning and power of these three words, just as Jesus felt when he said "And so it is!" at the end of a prayer or demonstration. You must intend those three words to do something, and in your case, you intend those three words to signify completion and closure.

When you say "It is done!" to yourself, feel deep within yourself the feelings of completion, satisfaction, peace, fulfillment and assurance. These are the closest words I can find to describe this feeling to you, so you must go within and seek your own feelings. How would you feel when something is done? How would you feel when a desire comes true for you, and there is nothing more that you have to do? How would you feel knowing that everything is already settled? That is the feeling we are gearing up for right here.

Notice that the feelings which you conjure up within yourself when you say, "It is done!" can be slightly different from the feelings you had when you visualized your desired outcome. When you visualized your desired outcome, your feelings were in response to the specifics of the situation. For example, I felt how I would feel when I queued up to collect my prize. That is a feeling of happiness, and also unique in the sense that it arose from me queuing up to collect my prize. However, in saying "it is done," the feeling we are going for is slightly different. The feeling is one of completion and fulfillment, in that something is already done and taken care of by the Universe. Therefore, there is no need for you to try and feel the same feelings as you did before in the first few steps. You do not need to "recall" how you felt earlier as you visualized. Simply focus on feeling the "it is done" feelings. What we are essentially looking for in the last step is a feeling of completion, ease and fulfillment.

Many books and teachers talk about how you should feel as if something has come to pass. When I read those teachings, I had an intellectual understanding and *knew* that was the way I was supposed to feel—but the books did not teach me how to feel that feeling. Thus, my intention is to explain, step-by-step and in a specific manner, what this "it is done" feeling entails.

When you say the phrase "It is done!" silently to yourself, use a triumphant tone of inner voice. Make it sound like a proclamation, a reflection of reality. Once again, if you have trouble doing this step or imagining what you would sound like, think back to a time when you told someone proudly that a task was completed. We've all had moments like this in our lives, so use your past successes here. How would you sound when you wanted to convey to a friend that something has been **done**—not just "in the process," but done! Settled! Fulfilled! What would your tone of voice sound like? Would it sound more like a wish—or more like a reflection of actual reality? That is the tonality we are going for.

Internalize this tone of voice and imagine yourself speaking it in your head. Imagine yourself making that proclamation that "It is done!" Next, as you are making that proclamation, feel the feelings associated with something being done, settled and complete. Feel the feelings of the Universal forces converging on your behalf and bringing whatever you want to you. The manifestation process which you did earlier has already set powerful Universal forces in action, and that is all you have to do! Your job is to set those Universal forces in motion with your intentions, by becoming clear over what your intentions are and then vibrating with that highest intent. The rest is up to the Universe, setting off a chain reaction and sequence of events that will bring what you want to you.

When you are feeling the "it is done" feeling, how long should you feel it for? I like to immerse myself in the feeling for what seems like a long time, but is actually fifteen to thirty seconds at most. Remember that fifteen to thirty seconds of vibrating at a pure, highly energized state with no interruptions works wonders in terms of the energy that you are actually moving. When this fifteen to thirty seconds of the "it is done" feeling is combined with what you have felt earlier in your manifestation process, the combined effect is very potent indeed, and can bring your manifestations to pass very quickly.

So feel the "it is done" feeling as you say the phrase, and then immerse yourself in the feeling for fifteen to thirty seconds. Sometimes you'll feel a "peak" in the feeling as I do; during which that feeling becomes so intense that my scalp and head actually twitches intensely! It is a very funny feeling that I can't properly describe, and what I think is happening is that I am shifting into a new possibility **at that very moment** and my physical body is literally accommodating those changes. I am moving into a new state of reality, where my desires and intentions are fulfilled, leaving the old state of reality behind. This shift is so profound to my physical body that it is still trying to "make sense" of this new state of reality.

When you use the "it is done" technique, you'll get to a point when you feel something which I call an "inner confirmation." This is an inner feeling where everything snaps into place, and you get a "confirmation" that it is truly done. This is a feeling of peace that surpasses all understanding. You just intuitively and deeply *know* that it is done. What I do is to feel those "it is done" feelings intensely, and usually about ten to fifteen seconds out, I get this "inner confirmation" that everything is done, and there is nothing more that I need to do. This is when I stop, and release everything.

By releasing everything, I mean that I completely and thoroughly let go of my intentions, desires, the outcome and the whole process. I don't even try to remember what I was asking for, or what I was doing just minutes earlier. I clear my mind and let it be free of deliberate thoughts.

Remember that there should not be any strain in any of this. If you are trying hard to feel that something is done, you're trying too hard! If you find yourself not easing into the process, you are trying too hard! Be easy on yourself. This is meant to be an intense and fun process. It is not meant to be additional work or strain for you. If you do it with the mindset of "I *have* to get it done correctly!" then things will be difficult for you. Instead, see yourself as playing with the energy field around you. See yourself as commanding the energy field when you say and feel the words "It is done!" For in that moment, it **is** done!

Try out the method as I have described above, and you'll find yourself experiencing many of the sensations I have described. You will recognize many of these sensations and feelings once you actually experience the exercise for yourself. Until then, reading about it is definitely no substitute. So put this book down and allow yourself to try this technique. Remember, it does not matter what manifestation technique you are currently using. This is a flexible method designed to complement whatever technique you have been using all along.

I've had individuals use it with great success with affirmations. They would write or state their affirmations, and then use the "it is done" technique at the very end. All of a sudden, they found affirmations becoming effective for them. In their case, there is no visualization involved but it still works, because the "it is done" technique is a feeling-based (experiential) process. I have had individuals use this technique along with vision boards. So they would look at their vision boards

RICHARD DOTTS

and then use the "it is done" technique right at the very end. The possibilities are endless, and I invite you to explore and play with them to see what new things you come up with.

One friendly reminder though, is that the "it is done" technique is extremely powerful—and I would not use it frivolously. It is alright to ask for whatever you really desire, such as an experience or a new outcome. However, it is *not* alright to "test" the Universe to make sure this really works. For example, after reading about the "it is done" technique, some may feel the need to "test" whether it works by frivolously applying the technique on intentions or desires which they do not particularly care for: "Since this technique is so powerful, just give me X!" Bear in mind that being imbued with creative powers is a huge responsibility, and that you are supposed to use this ability wisely to create that which you really want—instead of half-heartedly asking for things which you don't really care for. Therefore, don't adopt a flippant, "show me what you got" attitude with this technique. Treat the technique seriously and with respect, just as the ancient spiritual masters did when they too, used their own versions of this technique.

CHAPTER NINE
USING "IT IS DONE" IN OTHER SITUATIONS

In the final chapter of this book, I am going to talk about using the "it is done" technique in a variety of situations. The "it is done" technique is not only a useful manifestation aid, but it can also be used in times of crisis, emergencies, and for anything which you need urgent "help." I have found that using the "it is done" technique during emergency situations helps take the edge off things, and instantly calms and soothes my nerves.

In the past, before I discovered this method, I would be thrown into a panic each time I was faced with a last-minute, urgent situation that demanded my attention. For example, suppose that something went wrong at work and I had to set things right immediately, or that I realized I had lost something important. There are truly no limits to the "it is done" technique and how you can apply it. You can use it anytime and anywhere, because the Universe is always acting on your behalf. You have continuous access to powerful Universal forces, which are ready to help you out at any instant.

Let's talk about how to use the "it is done" technique for emergencies or urgent situations. Each time a crisis situation pops up, your mind will invariably think about all the worse possible scenarios and outcomes. Feelings of fear and worry may grip you. In times like this, I find it very useful to quickly envision the **opposite** of the undesired outcome. For example, if you have just lost a particular item, it is useful to immediately envision the opposite outcome, and imagine the item back in your possession once again. Or if you are facing an urgent situation at work, imagine the situation resolving itself and everything is back to normal. You may wish to phrase and state the desired outcome out loud as an intention statement. For example, "There is no loss in divine mind." Or, "Everything is working out for my highest good. Everything is resolved harmoniously." At the end of stating your highest and best intentions for the matter, finish off with "It is done!" and follow the steps described in the previous chapter. Feel the matter already resolved in that very moment, with nothing more that you have to do. Immerse yourself in the feeling until you get that "inner confirmation" that everything is alright.

Another effective way of using the "it is done" technique is for dealing with fears and worries that may just spontaneously pop up during the day. Suppose that you asked for your financial needs to be met, or for a particular situation to be resolved.

But throughout the day, worrying thoughts about that situation continue to surface in your mind. You may find yourself drifting to the problem several times over the course of the day. In the past, you would have had no choice but to accept this incessant worrying. Indeed, before I stumbled upon this technique, I had absolutely no way of handling all the worry- and fear-thoughts that popped up in my mind throughout the day! I could state my intentions and desires very clearly during my visualization and manifestation sessions, but I just had no way of handling all these distracting worry-thoughts that were popping up in my mind throughout the day.

Fortunately, you now have a straightforward and easy method to deal with these thoughts once they appear. Immediately affirm to yourself, "It is done!" and follow the steps given in the preceding chapter. As you say "it is done," feel the feelings of the problem completely solved or the issue resolved completely. Remember—you do not have to go into details or specifics of the problem, or envision the steps which are needed to resolve the problem. Skip any visualization of the problem situation completely. Instead, simply feel the finality and totality of it all, such that there is nothing else that you have to do. Feel that everything is already settled and moved into place by the powerful, omnipotent forces of the Universe. You have already stated your intentions very clearly and Universal forces are acting on them at this very moment, and there is nothing more you have to do! Through the "it is done" technique, you are reminding yourself of this fulfillment and perfection. You are focusing on a desired reality that already exists.

Do this as many times as necessary during the day, whenever worry- and fear-thoughts crop up into your mind. As you practice and become more familiar with the technique, you'll find that your worry- and fear-thoughts are no match for that empowering feeling and momentum when you go through the "it is done" process. I literally feel Universal forces and a great sense of momentum as I say the words "it is done," as well as a swirl of energy around myself, and goosebumps well up all over me. You'll find Universal forces converging so powerful on your behalf that your petty fears and worries simply are no match for them.

I have found the "it is done" method to be especially effective in dealing with fears, worries, distrust and impatience. These are the four main manifestation blocks we talked about in the first half of this book, and you can use the "it is done" technique to gently dissolve them.

Remember that the key is to **do this technique whenever these feelings crop up for you.** You have to get into the habit of dealing with these unwanted feelings each time they crop up for you, right on the spot, instead of waiting or deferring them until later. Too many people say something like, "Oh I'll deal with these feelings later, when I get off work..." but you'll be losing much of the useful benefits of this process if you do. The whole objective of the process is to give you a quick way to dissolve these four major manifestation blocks right when it matters.

How do you know when you have successfully dealt with these four major manifestation blocks in your life, and when they finally have become a thing of the past?

The surest indicator is that you'll feel light and free most of the time. You'll notice the *absence* of fear, worry, impatience or distrust in your life. Instead, your spontaneous thoughts will be of a happy and light nature. Therefore, the first sign that things are improving is that you'll worry less, and you'll start trusting the Universe more.

The second indicator that things are changing will be the speed and nature of your manifestations. You'll notice things happening for you a lot faster. You'll notice a decrease in the amount of time between a setting of intentions and actual manifestations. Things will begin happening very quickly for you, in such a way that you'll be able to pinpoint them accurately to your original intentions. More interestingly, things that you have wanted for a long time (some of which you may have forgotten having asked for) may begin happening for you! This is another sure sign that long-held resistance and blockages are starting to dissolve.

I remember a period in my life where many things started happening spontaneously for me. That was when I first dissolved these lifetime blockages in my life. I received many unexpected surprises and gifts—for example, receiving things and experiences that I had always wanted. It was only when I received the actual items (when the actual manifestations occurred) that I realized I had asked for these items before in the past, but had actually forgotten about them or given up on them!

The Universe keeps a perfect record and never forgets. You do not need to keep restating your intentions to the Universe as long as you state them clearly and purely the first time around. The moment you do, Universal forces are set into motion to bring your desires to you. My example is a perfect illustration of how the Universe does so, by delivering some of the things that I had asked for a long time ago. When you clear the blocks that are standing between you and your manifestations, long-held intentions will spontaneously come true for you.

Another sure sign that something is happening is that things will start happening for you even *before* you ask. I know this sounds counterintuitive, but it is certainly the case for me, now. Recently, I emailed a manufacturer to provide feedback about a faulty item I had purchased. Usually, this would be followed with a long exchange process where I have to provide details of the faulty product and ship it back, before it can be exchanged. To my surprise, the merchant shipped me a replacement unit immediately, which appeared directly in my mailbox—without me even have to say or do anything! The Universe always understands your full intentions and delivers them perfectly to you—**if you let it**. This has certainly been my experience, since letting go of these blocks.

Collectively, I think these experiences have taught me several powerful lessons. First of course, they reinforce the importance of letting go of the four major manifestation blocks. You must make a conscious decision to let them go today, and until you do, they will prevent your full manifestation abilities from shining through. They will prevent you from reaping the full benefits of these Universal principles. The moment you let go of your blocks completely, you'll find the Universe delivering your intentions and desires to you with remarkable accuracy and speed, *before* you even need to speak a word!

I encourage you to start putting the "it is done" technique to work in your life immediately. Do not delay. Work at dissolving the four major manifestation blocks in your life as they occur and then at implementing the "it is done" technique on a regular basis. Do it not just once or twice, but keep at it over the next few weeks and months until you see results. I promise that if you make these "it is done" principles a core tenet of your daily life, that you'll reap immense benefits and rewards from the process. You'll find yourself in amazement at how the Universe can deliver your requests to you so precisely and completely, with so little physical effort on your part. You'll be amazed, as I have, at how the

Universe understands your deepest intentions so perfectly—and brings what you want to you, at just the perfect time.

Most important, you'll discover—as I did—how the Universe operates with the purest and highest of intentions, with no ulterior motives, and that its only objective is to support your growth and well-being. Perhaps the closest word I can find to describe this indescribable feeling is one of unconditional love. Always remember that in the moment you intend something—**it is done! And so it is.** Now go live it like never before!

About The Author

Richard Dotts is a modern-day spiritual explorer. An avid student of ancient and modern spiritual practices, Richard shares how to apply these timeless principles in our daily lives. For more than a decade, he has experimented with these techniques himself, studying why they work and separating the science from the superstition. In the process, he has created successful careers as an entrepreneur, business owner, author and teacher.

Leading a spiritual life does not mean walking away from your current life and giving up everything you have. The core of his teachings is that you can lead a spiritual and magical life starting right now, from where you are, in whatever field you are in.

You can make a unique contribution to the world, because you are blessed with the abilities of a true creator. By learning how to shape the energy around you, your life can change in an instant, if you allow it to!

Richard is the author of more than 20 Amazon bestsellers on the science of manifestation and reality creation.

An Introduction to the Manifestations Approach of Richard Dotts

Even after writing more than 20 Amazon bestsellers on the subject of creative manifestations and leading a fulfilling life, Richard Dotts considers himself to be more of an adventurous spiritual explorer than a spiritual teacher or "master", as some of his readers have called him by.

"When you apply these spiritual principles in your own life, you will realize that everyone is a master, with no exceptions. Everyone has the power to design and create his own life on his own terms," says Richard.

"Therefore, there is no need to give up your power by going through an intermediary or any spiritual medium. Each time you buy into the belief that your good can only come through a certain teacher or a certain channel...you give up the precious opportunity to realize your own good. My best teachers were those who helped me recognize the innate power within myself, and kept the faith for me even when I could not see this spiritual truth for myself."

Due to his over-questioning and skeptical nature (unaided by the education which he received over the years), Richard struggled with the application of these spiritual principles in his early years.

After reading thousands of books on related subjects and learning about hundreds of different spiritual traditions with little success, Richard realized there was still one place left unexplored.

It was a place that he was the most afraid to look at: **his inner state.**

Richard realized that while he had been applying these Universal principles and techniques dutifully on the outside, his inner state remained tumultuous the whole time. Despite being well-versed in these spiritual principles, he was constantly plagued with negative feelings of worry, fear, disappointment, blame, resentment and guilt on the inside during his waking hours. These negative feelings and thoughts drained him of much of his energy and well-being.

It occurred to him that unless he was free from these negative feelings and habitual patterns of thought, any outer techniques he tried would not work. That was when he achieved his first spiritual breakthrough and saw improvements in his outer reality.

Taking A Light Touch

The crux of Richard's teachings is that one has to do the inner work first by tending to our own inner states. No one else, not even a powerful spiritual master, can do this for us. Once we have restored our inner state to a place of *zero*, a place of profound calmness and peace...that is when miracles can happen. Any subsequent intention that is held with <u>a light touch</u> in our inner consciousness quickly becomes manifest in our outer reality.

Through his books and teachings, Richard continually emphasizes the importance of taking a light touch. This means adopting a carefree, playful and detached attitude when working with these Universal Laws.

"Whenever we become forceful or desperate in asking for what we want, we invariably delay or withhold our own good. This is because we start to feel even more negative feelings of desperation and worry, which cloud our inner states further and prevent us from receiving what we truly want."

To share these realizations with others, Richard has written a series of books on various aspects of these manifestation principles and Universal Laws. Each of his books touches on a different piece of the manifestation puzzle that he has struggled with in the past.

For example, there are certain books that guide readers through the letting-go of negative feelings and the dropping of negative beliefs. There are books that talk about how to deal with self-doubt and a lack of faith in the application of these spiritual principles. Yet other books offer specific techniques for holding focused intentions in our inner consciousness. A couple of books deal with advanced topics such as nonverbal protocols for the manifestation process.

Richard's main goal is to break down the mysterious and vast subject of spiritual manifestations into easy to understand pieces for the modern reader. While he did not invent these Universal Laws and is certainly not the first to write about them, Richard's insights are valuable in showing readers how to easily apply these spiritual principles despite leading modern and hectic lifestyles. Thus, a busy mother of three or the CEO of a large corporation can just as easily access these timeless spiritual truths through Richard's works, as an ancient ascetic who lived quietly by himself.

It is Richard's intention to show readers that miracles are still possible in our modern world. When you experience the transformational power of these teachings for yourself, you stop seeing them as unexpected miracles and start seeing them as part of your everyday reality.

Do I have to read every book in order to create my own manifestation miracles?

Because Richard is unbounded by any spiritual or religious tradition, his work is continuously evolving based on a fine-tuning of his own personal experiences. He does, however, draw his inspiration from a broad range of teachings. Richard writes for the primary purpose of sharing his own realizations and not for any commercial interest, which is why he has shied away from the publicity that typically comes with being a bestselling author.

All of his books have achieved Amazon bestseller status with no marketing efforts or publicity, a testament to the effectiveness of his methods. An affiliation with a publishing house could mean a pressure to write books on certain popular subjects, or a need to censor the more esoteric and non-traditional aspects of his writing. Therefore, Richard has taken great steps to ensure his freedom as a writer. It is this freedom that keeps him prolific.

One of Richard's aims is to help readers apply these principles in their lives with minimal struggle or strain, which is why he has offered in-depth guidance on many related subjects. Richard himself has maintained that there is no need to read each and every single one of his books. Instead, one should just narrow in to the particular aspects that they are struggling with.

As he explains in his own words, "You can read just one book and completely change your life on the basis of that book if you internalized its teachings. You can do this not only with my books, but also with the books of any other author."

"For me, the journey took a little longer. One book could not do it for me. I struggled to overcome years of negative programming and critical self-talk, so much so that reading thousands of books did not help me as well. But after I reached that critical tipping point, when I finally 'got it', then I started to get everything. The first book, the tenth book, the hundredth book I read all started to make sense. I could pick up any book I read in the past and intuitively understand the spiritual essence of what the author was saying. But till I reached that point of understand within myself, I could not do so."

Therefore, one only needs to read as many books as necessary to achieve a true understanding on the inside. Beyond that, any reading is for one's personal enjoyment and for a fine-tuning of the process.

Which book should I start with?
There is no prescribed reading order. Start with the book that most appeals to you or the one that you feel most inspired to read. Each Richard Dotts book is self-contained and is written such that the reader can instantly benefit from the teachings within, no matter which stage of life they are at. If any prerequisite or background knowledge is needed, Richard will suggest additional resources within the text.

OTHER BOOKS
BY RICHARD DOTTS

M any of these titles are progressively offered in various formats (both in hard copy and eB-ook). Our intention is to eventually make all these titles available in hard copy format.

- **Banned Manifestation Secrets**
  It all starts here! In this book, Richard lays out the fundamental principles of spiritual manifes-tations and explains common misconceptions about the "Law of Attraction." This is also the book where Richard first talks about the impor-tance of one's inner state in creating outer manifestations.

- **Come and Sit With Me (Book 1): How to Desire Nothing and Manifest Everything**
  If you had one afternoon with Richard Dotts, what questions would you ask him about mani-festing your desires and the creative process? In Come and Sit With Me, Richard candidly answers some of the most pressing questions that have been asked by his readers. Written in a

free-flowing and conversational format, Richard addresses some of the most relevant issues related to manifestations and the application of these spiritual principles in our daily lives. Rather than shying away from tough questions about the manifestation process, Richard dives into them head-on and shows the readers practical ways in which they can use to avoid common manifestation pitfalls.

- **The Magic Feeling Which Creates Instant Manifestations**

  Is there really a "magic feeling", an inner state of mind that results in almost instant manifestations? Can someone live in a perpetual state of grace, and have good things and all your deepest desires come true spontaneously without any "effort" on your part? In this book, Richard talks about why the most effective part of visualizations lies in the *feelings*...and how to get in touch with this magic feeling.

- **Playing In Time And Space: The Miracle of Inspired Manifestations**

  In Playing In Time And Space, Richard Dotts shares the secrets to creating our own physical reality from our current human perspectives. Instead of seeing the physical laws of space and time as restricting us, Richard shares how anyone can transcend these perceived limitations of space and time by changing their thinking, and manifest right from where they are.

- **Allowing Divine Intervention**

  Everyone talks about wanting to live a life of magic and miracles, but what does a miracle really look like? Do miracles only happen to certain spiritual people, or at certain points in our lives (for example, at our most desperate)? Is it possible to lead an everyday life filled with magic, miracles and joy?

  In Allowing Divine Intervention, Richard explains how miracles and divine interventions are not reserved for the select few, but can instead be experienced by anyone willing to change their current perceptions of reality.

- **It is Done! The Final Step To Instant Manifestations**

  The first time Richard Dotts learnt about the significance of the word "Amen" frequently used in prayers…goosebumps welled up all over his body and everything clicked in place for him. Suddenly, everything he had learnt up to that point about manifestations made complete sense.

  In It Is Done!, Richard Dotts explores the hidden significance behind these three simple words in the English language. Three words, when strung together and used in the right fashion, holds the keys to amazingly accurate and speedy manifestations.

- **Banned Money Secrets**

  In Banned Money Secrets of the Hidden Rich, Richard explains how there is a group of individuals in our midst, coming from almost every

walk of life, who have developed a special rela-
tionship with money. These are the individuals
for whom money seems to flow easily at will,
which has allowed them to live exceedingly
creative and fulfilled lives unlimited by money.
More surprisingly, Richard discovered that there
is not a single common characteristic that unites
the "hidden rich" except for their unique ability
to focus intently on their desires to the exclusion of everything else. Some of the "hidden
rich" are the most successful multi-millionaires
and billionaires of our time, making immense
contributions in almost every field.

Richard teaches using his own life examples
that the only true, lasting source of abundance
comes from behaving like one of the hidden
rich, and from developing an extremely conducive inner state that allows financial abundance
to easily flow into your life.

- **The 95-5 Code: for Activating the Law of Attraction**
  Most books and courses on the Law of Attraction
  teach various outer-directed techniques one can
  use to manifest their desires. All is well and good,
  but an important question remains unanswered:
  What do you do during the remainder of your
  time when you are not actively using these manifestation techniques? How do you live? What do
  you do with the 95% of your day, the majority of
  your waking hours when you are not actively asking for what you want? Is the "rest of your day"
  important to the manifestation process?

It turns out that what you do during the 95% of your time, the time NOT spent visualizing or affirming, makes all of the difference.

In The 95-5 Code for activating the Law of Attraction, Richard Dotts explains why the way you act (and feel) during the majority of your waking hours makes all the difference to your manifestation end results.

- **Inner Confirmation for Outer Manifestations**
  How do you know if things are on their way after you have asked for them?

  What should you do after using a particular manifestation technique?

  What does evidence of your impending manifestations feel like?

  You may not have seen yourself as a particularly spiritual or intuitive person, much less an energy reader...but join Richard Dotts as he explains in Inner Confirmation for Outer Manifestations how everyone can easily perceive the energy fields around them.

- **Mastering the Manifestation Paradox**
  The Manifestation Paradox is an inner riddle that quickly becomes apparent to anyone who has been exposed to modern day Law of Attraction and manifestation teachings. It is an inner state that seems to be contradictory to the person practicing it, yet one that is associated with inevitably fast physical manifestations—that of *wanting* something and yet at the same time *not wanting* it.

Richard Dotts explains why the speed and timing of our manifestations depends largely on our mastery of the Manifestation Paradox. Through achieving a deeper understanding of this paradox, we can consciously and deliberately move all our desires (even those we have been struggling with) to a "sweet spot" where physical manifestations *have to occur* very quickly for us instead of having our manifestations happen "by default."

- **Today I Am Free: Manifesting Through Deep Inner Changes**
In Today I Am Free, Richard Dotts returns with yet another illuminating discussion of these timeless Universal Laws and spiritual manifestation principles. While his previous works focused on letting go of the worry and fear feelings that prevent our manifestations from happening in our lives, Today I Am Free focuses on a seldom discussed aspect of our lives that can affect our manifestations in a big way: namely our interaction with others and the judgments, opinions and perceptions that other people may hold of us. Richard Dotts shows readers simple ways in which they can overcome their constant feelings of fear and self-consciousness to be truly free.

- **Dollars Flow To Me Easily**
Is it possible to read and relax your way into financial abundance? Can dollars flow to you even if you just sat quietly in your favorite armchair and did "nothing"? Is abundance and prosperity

really our natural birthright, as claimed by so many spiritual masters and authors throughout the ages?

Dollars Flow To Me Easily takes an alternative approach to answering these questions. Instead of guiding the reader through a series of exercises to "feel as if" they are already rich, Richard draws on the power of words and our highest intentions to dissolve negative feelings and misconceptions that block us from manifesting greater financial abundance in our lives.

- **Light Touch Manifestations: How To Shape The Energy Field To Attract What You Want**

  Richard covers the entire manifestation sequence in detail, showing exactly how our beliefs and innermost thoughts can lead to concrete, outer manifestations. As part of his approach of taking a light touch, Richard shows readers how to handle each component of the manifestation sequence and tweak it to produce fast, effective manifestations in our daily lives.

- **Infinite Manifestations: The Power of Stopping at Nothing**

  In Infinite Manifestations, Richard shares a practical, step-by-step method for erasing the unconscious memories and blocks that hold our manifestations back. The Infinite Release technique, "revealed" to Richard by the Universe, is a quick and easy way to let go of any unconscious memories, blocks and resistances that may prevent our highest good from coming to us. When we invoke the Infinite Release process, we are no longer doing it alone. Instead, we step out of the way, letting go and letting God. We let Universal Intelligence decide how our inner resistances and blocks should be dissolved. All we need to do is to intend that we are clear from these blocks that hold us back. Once the Infinite Release process is invoked, it is done!

- **Let The Universe Lead You!**
  Imagine what your life would be like if you could simply hold an intention for something...and then be led clearly and precisely, every single time, to the fulfilment of your deepest desires. No more wondering about whether you are on the "right" path or making the "right" moves. No more second-guessing yourself or acting out of desperation—You simply set an intention and allow the Universe to lead you to it effortlessly!

- **Manifestation Pathways: Letting Your Good Be There...When You Get There!**
  Imagine having a desire for something and then immediately intuiting (knowing) what the path of least resistance should be for that desire. When you allow the Universe to lead you in this manner and unfold the manifestation pathway of least resistance to you, then life becomes as effortless as knowing what you want, planting it

in your future reality and letting your good be there when you get there...every single time! This book shows you the practical techniques to make it happen in your life.

- **And more...**

Made in the USA
Las Vegas, NV
29 April 2024

89304895R10066